NATURE'S LIGHT SHOW

THE NORTHERN LIGHTS

By Kristen Rajczak

 Gareth Stevens
Publishing

Please visit our website, www.garethstevens.com. For a free color catalog of all our high-quality books, call toll free 1-800-542-2595 or fax 1-877-542-2596.

Library of Congress Cataloging-in-Publication Data

Rajczak, Kristen.
The northern lights / Kristen Rajczak.
    p. cm. — (Nature's light show)
Includes index.
ISBN 978-1-4339-7028-3 (pbk.)
ISBN 978-1-4339-7029-0 (6-pack)
ISBN 978-1-4339-7027-6 (library binding)
1. Auroras—Juvenile literature. I. Title.
QC971.4.R35 2013
538'.768—dc23
                                    2011045161

First Edition

Published in 2013 by
Gareth Stevens Publishing
111 East 14th Street, Suite 349
New York, NY 10003

Designer: Katelyn E. Reynolds
Editor: Kristen Rajczak

Photo credits: Cover, p. 1, (cover, pp. 1, 3–24 background) Antony Spencer/Vetta/Getty Images; (cover, pp. 1, 3–24 graphics), pp. 4, 6, 8, 9, 12 Shutterstock.com; p. 5 Pekka Sakki/AFP/Getty Images; p. 7 Olivier Grunewald/Oxford Scientific/ Getty Images; pp. 11, 21 (inset) NASA; p. 13 Design Pics/Richard Wear/Getty Images; p. 14 NASA/Goddard Space Flight Center Scientific Visualization Studio; p. 15 Lodriguss Jerry/Photo Researchers/Getty Images; p. 17 Bob Hallinen/Anchorage Daily News/MCT via Getty Images; p. 18 NOAA/Newsmakers/Getty Images; p. 19 Space Frontiers/Hulton Archive/Getty Images; p. 20 iStockphoto/Thinkstock.com; p. 21 (main) Stocktrek Images/Arild Heitmann/Getty Images.

Printed in the United States of America

CPSIA compliance information: Batch #CS12GS: For further information contact Gareth Stevens, New York, New York at 1-800-542-2595.

CONTENTS

Stories of the Northern Lights 4

Auroras, Then and Now 6

Sun and Wind 8

Collision Course 10

Colors and Curtains 12

Close to the Pole 14

Extraordinary Auroras 16

Southern Lights 18

See the Light Show! 20

Glossary 22

For More Information 23

Index 24

Words in the glossary appear in **bold** type the first time they are used in the text.

STORIES OF THE NORTHERN LIGHTS

Beautiful, colorful lights in the skies have been observed for thousands of years. The explanations ancient people had for the lights' existence live on in stories all over the world. In Finland, they called these lights "fox fires" and believed fire foxes running in the mountains caused them. Others believed the lights were the spirits of dead people or animals.

Today, we call these lights auroras. The most famous auroras are called the aurora borealis, or northern lights.

The northern lights are a colorful sight.

Auroras were named after the Roman goddess of dawn, Aurora.

"Borealis" comes from the Greek god of the north wind, Boreas.

AURORAS, THEN AND NOW

During the 500s, colorful lights in the sky were said to be as bright as a day dawning. In 1621, **astronomers** Galileo Galilei and Pierre Gassendi first called these lights "aurora borealis" after seeing the lights flash and glow. "Aurora borealis" means "northern dawn."

Scientists today do much more than just watch auroras. They use special rockets and computers to study an aurora's activity. These studies have shown that the formation of an aurora starts with **charged** particles from the sun.

Galileo Galilei

EYE ON THE SKY

A particle is one of the small units that make up matter and energy.

Scientists study the northern lights to learn more about how auroras affect conditions on Earth.

7

SUN AND WIND

An aurora's formation begins when the sun shoots out a cloud of particles called plasma. Plasma is like a gas, but it has an electrical charge. **Solar** wind blows this cloud toward Earth.

When the plasma reaches Earth, it meets Earth's **atmosphere** and magnetic field. These play an important part in the formation of auroras. The magnetic field surrounding Earth pushes the charged particles toward the northern and southern **poles**. Then, particles **collide** with Earth's atmosphere.

This illustration shows how Earth's magnetic field pushes particles toward its poles.

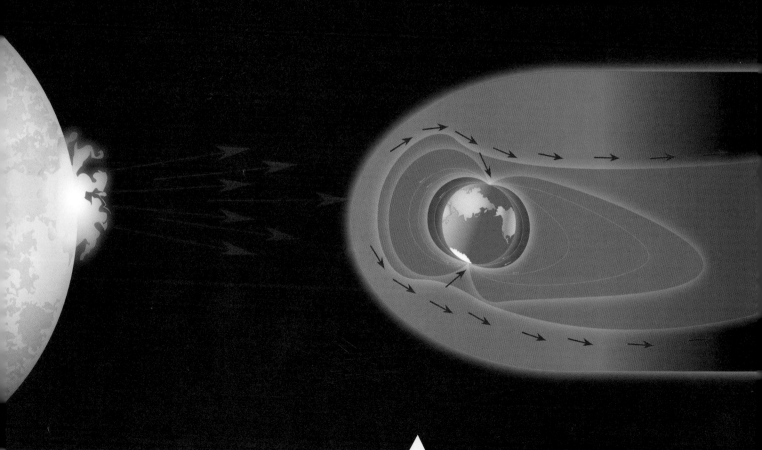

EYE ON THE SKY

The magnetic field around Earth can't be seen. However, it protects our planet by directing much of the solar wind away. Too many charged particles could be harmful to our atmosphere.

This picture shows solar wind traveling toward Earth, where it's mostly forced away by Earth's magnetic field.

COLLISION COURSE

The charged particles that enter Earth's atmosphere cause the colorful light of an aurora. Driven by energy from the sun, these particles move very fast. They collide with **atoms** in Earth's atmosphere, and the atoms take on some of this energy. The particles lose speed, too. As they slow, the particles collide with more atoms until their energy is gone.

Atoms have too much energy after colliding with the charged particles. This energy is released, and we see it as light.

EYE ON THE SKY

Earth's atmosphere is made up of many kinds of gas, including nitrogen, oxygen, argon, and carbon dioxide.

The collision of many particles and many atoms causes an aurora.

COLORS AND CURTAINS

Auroras appear as many shapes and colors. They may look like curtains or form arcs and bands of color across the sky. Faint auroras look like patches of glowing light.

Auroras commonly glow blue, purple, green, and yellow. Some **rare** auroras are red! An aurora's color depends on what kind of atoms the charged particles collide with. Oxygen **molecules** found about 60 miles (96.5 km) above Earth produce a yellow-green color. Oxygen atoms found 200 miles (322 km) above Earth cause red auroras. Nitrogen causes blue or purple lights.

These auroras seen over Iceland almost look like a rainbow!

Each aurora is special. You'll never see the same one twice!

EYE ON THE SKY

Some people report hearing sounds when an aurora occurs. However, scientists aren't sure the "whizzing" or "sparkling" sounds come from the aurora.

CLOSE TO THE POLE

The best places to see the northern lights are close to the North Pole. In fact, in places like Alaska, Greenland, and Norway, the lights can be seen many nights of the year. However, when the sun's activity increases, the aurora borealis becomes brighter and more colorful. During these times, it has been seen as far south as Mexico!

The northern lights are most easily seen between December and March. That's when nights near the North Pole are the longest and darkest.

Taken with a special camera, this picture shows what an aurora looks like from space.

Scientists say auroras go through a **cycle** of activity. Every 11 years, this cycle reaches its highest point, and the auroras are the most active.

It's possible to see an aurora from your house! This picture was taken in Philadelphia, Pennsylvania.

EXTRAORDINARY AURORAS

In February 1958, the skies in Alaska shone a bright, brilliant red. Scientists from all over the world were there as part of a yearlong study of Earth and its atmosphere. This rare red occurrence is said to be the most remarkable aurora of the 20th century!

A yellow-green aurora that appeared in March 1989 caught scientists' eyes, too. It was big—people as far south as Florida could see the glowing skies! Millions of people in Canada lost power because of magnetic storms the aurora caused.

Yellow green is one of the most common aurora colors.

EYE ON THE SKY

Magnetic storms are also called solar storms. Like auroras, they are caused by charged particles from the sun colliding with Earth's magnetic field.

17

SOUTHERN LIGHTS

Auroras occurring near the South Pole are called the southern lights, or aurora australis. They are caused by the same solar winds and collision of particles that cause the northern lights. In fact, the southern lights often happen at the same time and with shapes and colors similar to the northern lights.

However, the southern lights are less likely to be seen. They commonly take place over the Indian Ocean and Antarctica, a continent too cold and icy for people to live there.

Sometimes, the southern lights can be seen from southern Australia.

In September 2011, astronauts recorded a video of the southern lights from the International Space Station.

"Australis" is Latin for "of the south."

19

What's that on the horizon—a cloud or a faint aurora? If you can see stars through it, it's an aurora!

The closer to the North Pole you travel, the brighter the northern lights will be. To best see the beautiful lights, it must be very dark, the weather must be calm, and the skies clear. Late night and early morning are the best viewing times. Watch the sky carefully. Auroras often only last 10 to 30 minutes, and you won't want to miss a moment!

Some people camp out to see the northern lights!

HOW DOES AN AURORA FORM?

1. The sun releases a cloud of charged particles.

2. Solar wind pushes the particles toward Earth.

3. Earth's magnetic field directs the particles to its poles.

4. Particles collide with atoms in the atmosphere, passing on energy.

5. Atoms light up as they release the extra energy.

GLOSSARY

astronomer: a person who studies the movements and makeup of the stars, planets, and other heavenly bodies

atmosphere: the gases surrounding Earth

atom: the smallest unit that makes up matter

charged: filled with electricity

collide: the hitting of two objects against each other

cycle: a series of events that repeat in the same order

molecule: a small unit of matter made up of atoms

pole: the top or bottom of Earth

rare: not common

solar: having to do with the sun

FOR MORE INFORMATION

Books

Bodden, Valerie. *Northern Lights.* Mankato, MN: Creative Education, 2010.

Bow, James. *Earth Mysteries Revealed.* New York, NY: Crabtree Publishing, 2010.

Lynch, Wayne. *Arctic A to Z.* Richmond Hill, Ontario, Canada: Firefly Books, 2009.

Websites

Patterns in Nature: Aurorae
photography.nationalgeographic.com/photography/photos/patterns-aurorae/
Look through this picture gallery to see many different aurora colors and formations.

The Space Place
spaceplace.nasa.gov/
Learn more about cool space happenings like the northern lights. Play games and solve puzzles, too.

INDEX

Alaska 14, 16

Antarctica 18

atmosphere 8, 9, 10, 16, 21

atoms 10, 11, 12, 21

Aurora (goddess) 5

aurora australis 18

aurora borealis 4, 6, 14

Australia 18

Boreas 5

charged particles 6, 8, 9, 10, 11, 12, 17, 18, 21

collide 8, 10, 11, 12, 17, 18, 21

colors 4, 6, 10, 12, 14, 16, 17, 18

cycle 15

energy 10, 21

Florida 16

fox fires 4

Galilei, Galileo 6

Gassendi, Pierre 6

Greenland 14

magnetic field 8, 9, 17, 21

magnetic storms 16, 17

Mexico 14

North Pole 14, 20

Norway 14

plasma 8

poles 8, 21

shapes 12, 18

solar wind 8, 9, 18, 21

sounds 13

southern lights 18, 19

South Pole 18

spirits 4

sun 6, 8, 10, 14, 17, 21